WORLD OF KANDY - UKRAINE

From Ukraine with Love
Olga Maria

Birthday August 19th
Height 170cm
Weight 60kg
Eyes Green
Hair Dark brown
Instagram @olgamaria_veide
Favorite Movie The Great Gatsby
Favorite Band Boombox

Photos Kopenick Studio

Where are you from and what's it like in your country? I am from Ukraine. The most beautiful girls come from here.

What are your hobbies? There are many things I like to do in my free time and I never feel bored. I like to do yoga, walk in nature, explore new things, and improve my skills.

Have you ever been to America? I have never been to America, but I hope to explore that beautiful country someday.

SPRING 2025 | © KANDY MAGAZINE

TABLE OF CONTENTS

KANDY SPRING 2025

COVER MODEL

DJ AMIE ROSE
SPINNING HER WAY TO THE TOP

In the words of the immortal Donna Summer, DJ Amie Rose loves the nightlife baby. Sit back and enjoy Amies' voyeuristic Kandy pictorial.

What's Inside

Celebrity Feature
Stacey Hayes

We first met Stacey a long time ago at a Vince Neil charity golf event. She was one of the girls beautifying the scenery around hole 9. Since then, she shot to stardom as the co-host of the original game show Lingo.

Kandystand Sweet
Gia Ramey-Gay

It is hard to say no to a girl and candy. Especially one that is talented enough to blow a heart shaped bubble. No photoshop necessary.

Formula 1
2025 Season Forecast

Sports fans, we lead with Formula 1. It is a season that will be filled with drama. Lewis Hamilton heads over to Ferrari. All is not well on Team McLaren - a Lando Norris / Oscar Piastri feud is brewing.

Make Checks Out to:
Kandy Enterprises LLC
7260 W. Azure Dr. Ste 140-639
Las Vegas, NV 89130
Yes! I want KANDY! SEND ME:

6 issues for $60 (1 Year)

12 issues for $96 (2 Years)

First Name

Last Name

Street Address

Street Address

City

State

Zip Code

Payment Enclosed
Please allow 4 to 6 weeks
for delivery of first issue.

For Credit card, Paypal and
other payment options
go to https://kandy.store

SPRING 2025

EDITOR'S LETTER

Spring is here! And that means sports. Is there a better time of the year for a sports fan? For starters, there is the NCAA Men's basketball tournament. There will be no UConn 3-peat. Coach Hurley should have taken that Lakers' gig. Are we looking at a National Champion out of the SEC this year? Auburn and Alabama are making a strong case to be the ones cutting down the nets in April. Lest us not forget the NBA. Well, actually, we defecate all over the current iteration of the National Basketball Association. Why? In 4 words - Lebron, Curry, Kerr, Pop. That should tell you everything you need to know. And before you get up on your pedestal, let us set the record straight. We were huge NBA fans. So big, we have a couple columns inside dedicated to the league's hey-day - the 1980s where Magic and Bird were fierce rivals. The Pistons mugged their way to a crown and Dr. J, Patrick Ewing and Bernard King were supporting players that in today's NBA would your nightly ESPN headliners.

Are you a auto racing fan? We are pulling serious Gs inside. First up, the 2025 Formual 1 circuit. Is this the year Lando Norris knocks Max off his pedestal? Will Lewis Hamilton migrating to Ferrari bring a Constructor's championship to Scuderia Ferrari? Are you more a NASCAR guy? Man, was that some Daytona 500 or what? We break down our view of the remainder of the season. What about IndyCar? We take you back to what we believe was its greatest ERA - the 1970s where the legends of Rick Mears, AJ Foyt, and Bobby Unser were made.

Spring is not complete without MLB. 2025 will be an exciting season in baseball. There are a few rule changes. Spring Training games have MLB testing the new ABS (ball-strike) system. Younger players love it, older guys not so much. The Mets spent big on Soto; the Dodgers made a mockery of the league's salary cap with the exploitation of "deferred salary".

We kick off our dedication to sports with a Hollywood crossover - the Formula 1 racing films feud between Steve McQueen and James Garner. It is a fascination story. We hope you enjoy our retelling.

Of course, no issue of Kandy is complete without the ladies. Leading off is our cover girl, DJ Amie Rose. I bet that cover grabbed your attention. She is joined inside by Gia who loves her some Kandy. Our celebrity spotlight is former Lingo gameshow co-host Stacey Hayes. As she said on the Howard Stern once, that's with two e's and two y's. Yes, indeed Stacey, yes indeed.

Cheers!

Ron Kuchler

SPRING 2025 | © KANDY MAGAZINE

ENTERTAINMENT

SPORTS

WOMEN

MEN'S LIFESTYLE

Editor in Chief
Ron Kuchler

Managing Editor
Dave Packo

Contributing Photographers
Mike Prado, Mario Barberio, WJR Parks

Stock Credits
Giants Field Photo by Mick Haupt / Unsplash
Peoria Spring Training Photo by Megan Ellis / Unsplash
Dodger stadium Photo by Sung Shin / Unsplash
Citifield Photo by Tomas Eidsvold / Unsplash
Basketball rack Photo by Todd Greene / Unsplash
LA Court Photo by Tim Hart on Unsplash
Daytona 500 John K Harrelson NKP Courtesy Team Penske

Contact Us
Kandy Enterprises LLC
7260 W Azure Dr. Ste 140-639
Las Vegas, NV 89130
www.kandymag.com
Facebook @kandymagazine
X @kandy_magazine
Instagram @kandymagazine

General Inquiries - info@kandymag.com
Letters to The Editor - letters@kandymag.com
Copyright - legal@kandymag.com
Subscription Inquiries - subscriptions@kandymag.com

Spring 2025
KANDY MAGAZINE
© 2025 Kandy Enterprises LLC.
All Rights Reserved.

KANDYMAG.COM

A DAY IN THE LIFE OF

STACEY HAYES

✦✦✦

PHOTOS BY
MARIO BARBERIO

SPRING 2025 | © KANDY MAGAZINE

KANDY CELEBRITY

Have you ever wondered what a typical day would look like for a Hollywood starlet? Well, actress and TV host Stacey Hayes gives us a glimpse in her Kandy pictorial. Stacey's day encompasses a morning photo shoot in a 1979 Cadillac Eldorado with original turquoise paint and interior. After a quick bike ride around the neighborhood Stacey cools off with a dip in the pool. Ah, life in paradise. Let's take a look.

KANDY CELEBRITY

Facts About Stacey
She hosted a show in the U.K., called "Stepping Out the Glamorous Life" where she took viewers inside exclusive U.K. VIP clubs/ parties.

Stacey is best known for co-hosting the original Lingo game show with Chuck Woolery.

SPRING 2025 | © KANDY MAGAZINE

KANDY SPORTS GUY

The 2025 Formula 1 Season
A New Era of Chaos and Champions

CHARLES LECLERC, Scuderia Ferrari SF-25 - Photo Florent Gooden / DPPI

As the engines roar to life for the 2025 Formula 1 season, kicking off with the Australian Grand Prix on March 16, we're staring down the barrel of what could be one of the most unpredictable and exhilarating campaigns in recent memory. The 2024 season gave us a taste of parity - McLaren snagged the Constructors' Championship, Max Verstappen clung to his Drivers' title, and Ferrari emerged as a late-season juggernaut. Now, with the grid reshuffled, rookies aplenty, and the final year of the current regulations before the 2026 overhaul, 2025 promises a wild ride. Here's my take on the drivers, teams, and storylines that'll define this 75th anniversary season - complete with predictions bold enough to make even Guenther Steiner raise an eyebrow.

The Big Four: A Championship Free-for-All
The top of the heap looks like a four-way cage match between McLaren, Ferrari, Red Bull, and Mercedes, each with firepower to dominate - or implode.

KANDY SPORTS GUY

MCLAREN
Lando Norris & Oscar Piastri

Fresh off their Constructors' triumph, McLaren enters 2025 as the team to beat. Norris, who fell agonizingly short of the Drivers' title in 2024 (second to Verstappen), has the pace, maturity, and hunger to go one better. Piastri, the cool-headed Aussie, proved his mettle with two wins last year and could easily play spoiler - or champion - if McLaren's MCL39 successor keeps its edge. Their 2024 car was a rocket after Miami upgrades; if they nail the winter development (a historical weak spot), they're my pick to repeat as Constructors' champs.

Prediction: Norris wins the Drivers' Championship, McLaren takes Constructors' again. Friction between Norris and Piastri from 2024 boils over in 2025 leading to a separation once the season concludes The papaya dynasty ends before it even begins.

LEWIS HAMILTON, Scuderia Ferrari SF-25 - Photo Florent Gooden / DPPI

FERRARI
Charles Leclerc & Lewis Hamilton

Ferrari's late-2024 surge - outscoring everyone post-Monaco - sets the stage for a seismic season. Leclerc, operating at peak form (most points after the Dutch GP), is my dark horse for the Drivers' title. Then there's Hamilton, the seven-time champ, swapping Silver Arrows for rosso corsa. At 40, he's out to silence doubters and snag that elusive eighth title. Fred Vasseur's "99% new" Project 677 car sounds like a beast; if it delivers, Ferrari could end their 17-year Constructors' drought. But can Leclerc and Hamilton coexist without fireworks?

Prediction: Leclerc edges Hamilton for second in Drivers', Ferrari wins Constructors' if they avoid strategy blunders.

SPRING 2025 | © KANDY MAGAZINE

KANDY SPORTS GUY

RED BULL
Max Verstappen & Liam Lawson

Verstappen's a machine - four straight titles, unflappable under pressure (437 points in 2024 despite a wobbly RB20). But Red Bull's aura took a hit last year: Adrian Newey's exit (he's Aston Martin-bound), a Constructors' fade to third, and Sergio Pérez's collapse (parted ways post-Abu Dhabi). Enter Liam Lawson, the 22-year-old Kiwi with 11 races of grit under his belt. He's no Verstappen, but he's feisty - think Mexico 2024, tangling with Pérez. Red Bull's hopes hinge on the RB21 recapturing lost mojo.

Prediction: Verstappen takes third in Drivers', Red Bull slips to fourth in Constructors'. Lawson podiums thrice.

MERCEDES
George Russell & Kimi Antonelli

Russell outshone Hamilton in 2024 (two wins, 235 points), cementing his status as Mercedes' alpha. Now paired with 18-year-old Kimi Antonelli, a prodigy skipping F3 entirely, the Silver Arrows are rolling the dice. Antonelli's raw speed is undeniable - F2 wins in a tough field - but F1's brutality could expose his inexperience. Mercedes' W16 needs to leap forward from 2024's fourth-place finish (409 points).

Prediction: Russell snags fifth in Drivers', Antonelli grabs a podium, Mercedes lands third in Constructors'.

The Midfield Maulers Upsets in Waiting

The chasing pack is tighter than ever, with six rookies and savvy veterans ready to pounce on any Big Four slip-ups.

Williams: Alex Albon & Carlos Sainz

Sainz's move from Ferrari to Williams is the off-season's sleeper hit. A four-time winner (most recently Australia 2024), he brings savvy to a team on the rise, paired with Albon's underrated brilliance. Williams sniffed points regularly in 2024; with Sainz, they could steal a podium - or a win in chaos like Brazil 2023.

Prediction: Sainz ninth, Albon 13th, Williams jumps to sixth in Constructors'.

Aston Martin Fernando Alonso & Lance Stroll
Alonso, 43, still has the fire (eight podiums in 2023), but Aston's 2024 fade (fifth, 296 points) exposed their limits. Newey arrives midseason, too late for a 2025 miracle, but Enrico Cardile's influence might lift them. Stroll's consistency remains the wildcard.

Prediction: Alonso 12th, Stroll 16th, Aston holds fifth in Constructors'.

Haas Oliver Bearman & Esteban Ocon

Bearman, the 19-year-old Ferrari protégé, dazzled in Jeddah 2024 (P7 subbing for Sainz), while Ocon's pedigree (Hungary 2021 win) adds steel. Haas climbed to seventh in 2024; this duo could push them higher.

Prediction: Ocon 11th, Bearman 14th, Haas leaps to seventh in Constructors'.

Alpine
Pierre Gasly & Jack Doohan

Gasly's double podium in Brazil 2024 showed Alpine's potential, but 2025 is their last dance with Renault engines. Doohan, the F2 standout, steps up as a rookie. Expect flashes, not fireworks.

Prediction: Gasly 10th, Doohan 18th, Alpine drops to ninth.

Racing Bulls (RB)
Yuki Tsunoda & Isack Hadjar

Tsunoda's speed is legit (50 points in 2024), but Red Bull snubbed him for Lawson. Hadjar, F2 runner-up, is raw but rapid. RB's eighth-place finish (46 points) could improve - or stagnate.

Prediction: Tsunoda 15th, Hadjar 19th, RB stays eighth.

Sauber
Nico Hülkenberg & Gabriel Bortoleto

Hülkenberg's experience (227 starts, no podiums) meets Bortoleto's F2 title-winning youth. Sauber's dismal 2024 (zero points) needs a miracle before Audi's 2026 arrival.

Prediction: Hülkenberg 17th, Bortoleto 20th, Sauber languishes in 10th.

Wild Cards and Subplots
Rookie Surge

Six newcomers - Antonelli, Lawson, Bearman, Doohan, Hadjar, and Bortoleto - flood the grid. Bet on at least two podiums, with Bearman and Antonelli the likeliest.

Hamilton vs. Leclerc

Will Ferrari's dream team spark or sputter? Hamilton's racecraft might outshine Leclerc's qualifying edge, but egos could clash.

Regulation Finale

Teams might throw curveballs in this last year before 2026's reset - think flexi-wing controversies or engine rows.

Podium Parity

2024 saw 10 drivers on the rostrum; We predict 11 in 2025, with Ocon or Sainz sneaking in.

Final Predictions Drivers' Championship

1. Lando Norris
2. Charles Leclerc
3. Max Verstappen
4. Lewis Hamilton
5. George Russell

Constructors' Championship

1. McLaren
2. Ferrari
3. Mercedes
4. Red Bull
5. Aston Martin

Surprise of the Season

Haas cracks the top six in Constructors'.

Bust of the Season

Red Bull's Lawson experiment falters, prompting midseason murmurs of a Tsunoda swap.

This season's a powder keg - veterans chasing glory, rookies hunting headlines, and teams teetering between triumph and turmoil. McLaren's got the momentum, Ferrari's got the romance, and Verstappen's still the benchmark. Strap in; 2025's about to go full throttle.

KANDY SPORTS GUY

The Golden Age of Formula 1
The 1980s, Where Speed Met Soul

In the annals of Formula 1, no era shines brighter, burns hotter, or lingers longer in the collective heartbeat of the sport than the 1980s. It was a decade of unbridled romance - an era when machines roared with untamed fury, drivers danced on the edge of mortality, and the racetrack was a canvas for legends to paint their immortality. Turbocharged engines screamed like banshees. Circuits gleamed with danger. Rivalries smoldered with a passion that turned asphalt into poetry. Some call it F1's greatest era, a love affair between man, machine, and destiny that we'll never see again - and perhaps never should.

The Symphony of Speed

Picture it: the mid-1980s, where turbo engines - those wild, fire-breathing beasts—pushed cars to over 1,000 horsepower in qualifying trim. The Renaults, Ferraris, and BMWs didn't just accelerate; they erupted, hurling drivers down straights like comets trailing sparks. Tracks like Monza, Hockenheim, and the old Österreichring were cathedrals of velocity, their long, sweeping lines echoing with the howl of mechanical gods. Qualifying laps weren't races - they were duels with physics, drivers wringing every ounce of power from engines that could grenade at any moment. Gilles Villeneuve once said, "I don't drive to finish; I drive to feel alive." That was the '80s—alive, raw, and reckless.

The cars themselves were works of art, sculpted in carbon fiber and aluminum, kissed by the genius of designers like Gordon Murray and John Barnard. The McLaren MP4/4, a blood-red-and-white masterpiece, dominated in 1988, winning 15 of 16 races. The Lotus 97T, painted in John Player Special black and gold, danced through corners like a ballerina with a death wish. These cars weren't sanitized machines; they smoked, shuddered, and broke. And in their imperfection lay their beauty.

The Knights of the Circuit

The drivers of this era were knights-errant, armed not with swords but with courage that bordered on madness. Alain Prost, the Professor, wove his races with a mathematician's precision, his four titles (1985, '86, '89) a testament to a mind as sharp as his throttle control. Ayrton Senna, the mystic warrior, drove with a divine fury - his wet-weather wizardry at Monaco '84 and Donington '93 still whispers of the supernatural. Nelson Piquet, the sly fox, snagged three crowns (1981, '83, '87) with a blend of guile and grit, while Nigel Mansell, the lionheart, threw his Williams into corners with a desperation that won hearts if not always races.

Their rivalries were operatic. Prost vs. Senna - the cerebral Frenchman against the soulful Brazilian - was F1's biggest love-hate saga. Their 1989 Suzuka crash, Senna disqualified after pushing Prost off, and the 1990 rematch, Senna ramming Prost to clinch the title, were acts of passion as much as aggression. It was betrayal, vengeance, and genius colliding at 200 mph. Piquet vs. Mansell at Williams in '86-'87 was quieter but no less fierce - teammates who'd sooner sabotage each other than share glory. These weren't just races; they were duels of destiny, fought with a ferocity that made the podium feel like a throne.

The Dance with Danger
Romance demands risk, and the 1980s delivered it in spades. The final era before safety was king - tracks like Imola, Brands Hatch, and the old Spa-Francorchamps were unforgiving lovers, their barriers close, their runoffs scarce. Drivers flirted with death weekly; some didn't come back. Gilles Villeneuve's fiery end at Zolder in 1982, Riccardo Paletti's tragedy in Canada that same year, and the near-misses - like Didier Pironi's career-ending crash at Hockenheim—cast a shadow over the glamour. Yet that danger fueled the allure. Every lap was a tightrope walk, every victory a triumph over fate.

The fans knew it as well. Grandstands overflowed with devotees who didn't just watch - they felt. The Tifosi at Monza wept and cheered as Ferrari's scarlet cars roared past, turbo lag cast aside to irrelevancy. Monaco's streets shimmered with the jet-set, but the real stars were the drivers threading the needle through Armco-lined turns. Silverstone's roar, Kyalami's dust - it was a global romance, a sport that seduced continents.

The Twilight of Titans
By 1989, the turbo era faded - FIA banned the monsters, ushering in the 3.5-liter naturally aspirated engines of the '90s. The MP4/4's 15-1 season was the crescendo, a swan song for an age of excess. But what a song it was. The 1980s gave us 10 seasons of unrelenting drama: Prost's tactical brilliance, Senna's pole-position artistry (65 in his career), Mansell's mustache-and-moxie charge to the 1992 title after years of near-misses. It was the last gasp of a Formula 1 unbound by today's simulators, sensors, and sanitized rivalries.

Why It Was the Greatest
The 1980s weren't perfect - crashes were too common, politics too messy (think FISA vs. FOCA) - but that's why they were perfect. It was F1 with soul, where drivers weren't corporate robots but poets of speed, where cars weren't data-driven drones but temperamental lovers. It was Senna praying in the cockpit, Prost plotting in the pits, and Piquet smirking through the chaos. It was noise, danger, and dreams colliding in a haze of exhaust and glory.

Today's F1 is faster, safer, and slicker - but it'll never recapture that raw romance. The 1980s were a fleeting affair, a decade when the sport burned brightest because it danced closest to the flame. We'll chase its ghost forever, and that's the sweetest heartbreak of all.